Manual for Buglers

How to Play the Bugle and Practice the Calls and Marching Songs Used in the United States Military

By the U. S. Navy

Adansonia Press

Published in 2018

Logo art adapted from work by Bernard Gagnon

ISBN-13: 978-0-359-01211-4

First published in 1919

Reprinted in 1951 and 1953 with minor corrections

Contents

Preface .... *iv*

Chapter One – The Bugler 5

Chapter Two - Sounding the Bugle 11

Chapter Three - Reading Music 21

Chapter Four - Starting Your Practice 37

Chapter Five - Bugle Practice 43

Chapter Six - The Calls 52

Preface

This book is one of the series of Navy Training Courses, and has been written to help the Bugler to learn his duties in minimum time. Ordinarily, the Bugler is a Seaman under the direction of a Quartermaster who may or may not have been a Bugler himself. Since the Bugler is frequently on his own in learning music notation and the technique of playing the bugle, this book has been designed for self-study.

It contains complete instructions for playing the bugle, as well as a complete list of the bugle calls authorized for use in the Navy. Every effort has been made to notate calls as they have been traditionally sounded in the Navy. New exercises have been written for the present edition to replace those found in chapters 4 and 5 of earlier printings.

The Manual for Buglers, US Navy, was prepared by the US Navy Training Publications Center with cooperation, assistance, and technical review by the US Navy School of Music, Naval Receiving Station, Washington, DC

Chapter One – The Bugler

The Bugler is a mighty important man in the US Navy. On board ship the bugle sounds a warning call for almost every activity in which a group of men is to take part. You are probably already familiar with a number of these calls, such as "Reveille," "Mess call," "Evening Colors," and "Taps." These are but four of more than 100 bugle calls used in the Navy, including a few which are used only in emergencies, such as "Man overboard" or "Abandon ship."

Before the days of electrical communication systems the bugle was one of the few means by which orders could be sent from the quarter deck to any section of the ship. On small ships a single bugle could be heard everywhere on the ship, while on larger vessels sometimes as many as two or three additional Buglers were used to relay the calls down the hatches and into remote parts of the ship.

Even now, with all our modern methods of communication, the bugle is traditionally the means employed to render honors, to attract the attention of the men for a special announcement, or to signal the routine of the day.

The use of the bugle or a similar instrument as a military signaling device dates back many centuries, probably originating when someone discovered that a cow's or sheep's horn would make a noise when air was blown through it. Down through the ages many improvements were made on these military instruments. No doubt, the first was the substitution of metal for the animal's horn. This permitted more careful design of the instruments and, since the metal could be formed into almost any shape, it led to a study of the proper size and shape of the tube to produce a pleasing sound.

Before the bugle was as well developed as it is now, no one attempted to play a standard call on his instrument. Each player invented his own call and his skill was judged by the loudness of his blasts.

As the instrument has improved, so have the calls. The skills involved in sounding the calls have also changed. Because the calls have progressed beyond single tone blasts to take their place as melodic compositions, mere loudness is no longer considered a standard of excellence. Today, tone quality, rhythm, and intonation (playing notes which are in tune—neither too high, nor too low) are considered much more important to you as a Bugler, than the amount of noise that you can make.

It might be well to mention here that a bugle is sounded, not blown. Remember—you can blow a ram's horn, but it takes more than blowing to sound your bugle.

The regulation bugle which you have been issued is made of brass and is built in the key of G. You will not have to worry about the key of the bugle because the bugle is used only as a solo instrument or in a drum and bugle corps and the key is important only when a number of different kinds of instrument play together.

The bugle has five important parts, the mouthpiece, the tube or coils, the bell tube, the bell, and the tuning slide.

The MOUTHPIECE is usually made of brass, and plated with gold, silver, or chromium. It may look as though its only function is to serve as an air funnel, but it has another important job. It catches the vibrations produced by your lips and carries them into the air column inside the bugle. It is the vibration of this air column which makes the sound that you hear. Actually, all sound is made up of vibrations.

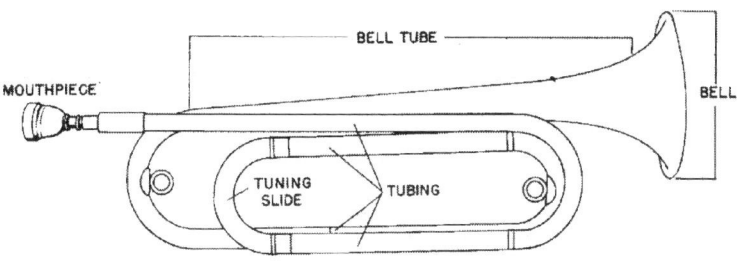

Figure 1-1. — The bugle.

The cup of the regulation mouthpiece is always the same size and shape. Some Buglers, whose lips do not fit comfortably in the regulation mouthpiece, prefer to use a commercial trumpet mouthpiece. This is a matter for you to decide; however, it is a good idea, once you have found a mouth piece which fits your lips satisfactorily, always to use this same mouthpiece.

The TUBE is the part of the instrument which has the same diameter for its entire length of about four feet. The length and, to a lesser degree, the diameter of the tube of any instrument determine the highest and lowest note which can be sounded on that instrument. This is because a long air column vibrates slower than a short one.

The BELL is the wide portion at the end of the bugle which acts like a megaphone to spread the tone. The bell tapers into the bell tube, which is the portion of the tubing with the constantly increasing diameter.

The TUNING SLIDE can be found in the mouthpiece end of the shortest coil on your bugle and is used, as its name indicates, to tune the instrument. When the slide is pushed all the way in, the bugle plays in the key of G. Drawing the slide out lengthens the tube and lowers the sound of the notes which can be played. The slide can be drawn out about three and a half inches. A letter F engraved on the lower sleeve of the slide indicates the approximate setting for the slide so that you can play calls written in the key of F. This means that every note on the bugle will be lowered one full step in the musical scale. Normally, the key of F is used only when a drum and bugle corps is playing with a band.

Like all of your gear, the bugle must be properly cared for to give the best results. At least once a week, you should clean the inside with hot, soapy water. Rinse the instrument out well and shake all of the water out carefully. Grease the slide with vaseline or cosmoline to prevent corrosion of the metal and to keep the slide free to move.

Bugles which have a lacquered finish are cleaned on the outside by wiping them with a damp cloth. Bugles with a plain brass finish, or those on which the lacquer is badly worn, should be polished with bright work polish. Remember that this polish will remove the lacquer.

When the plating on your mouthpiece wears thin, it should be replated since the brass is harder to keep free of germs than the plating material; in addition, brass has a very poor taste. The replating can be done on most repair ships, or a local music store can return the mouthpiece to the factory for the job.

You can prevent too frequent replating jobs by handling the mouthpiece carefully. When you remove it from the bugle don't set it cup-down on any rough surface. Make a habit of laying the mouthpiece on its side to avoid nicks in the rim of the cup. This rim is in constant contact with your lips when you play and nicks or scratches on it will chafe your skin.

The tube of the mouthpiece can be cleaned by using a heavy-tufted pipe-cleaner, or a thin wooden stick and a clean piece of cloth. It is best not to use wire or any metal object to push the cloth through since you may scratch the cup this way.

The Positions of a Bugler

The position which you should use when you are sounding a call is discussed in detail in the next chapter on "Sounding the Bugle." Other positions to be used when you are standing inspection, marching, or saluting are shown in figures 1-2 to 1-7.

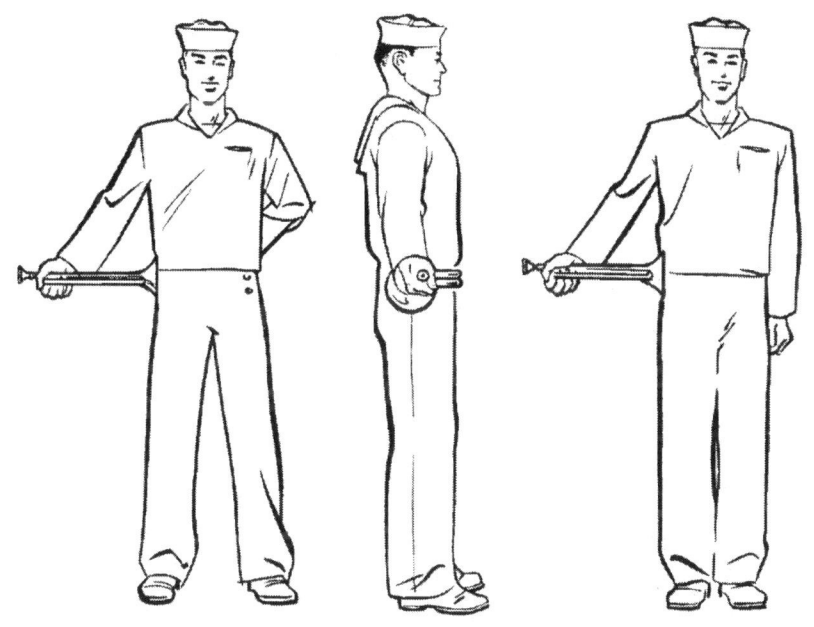

Figure 1-2. - Attention; Figure 1-3. - Carry bugle; Figure 1-4. - Parade rest.

Figure 1-5. - Secure bugle; Figure 1-6. - Bugle salute; Figure 1-7. Inspection bugle.

Chapter Two - Sounding the Bugle

By this time you have probably tried the bugle on for size, so to speak. You may have had good results in your first attempt, or perhaps you've had nothing but grunts thus far. No matter how successful you've been in your early efforts, you are going to need plenty of practice to be able to sound the bugle calls properly. But, before you begin your practice, you will profit by reading and understanding the instructions which follow.

POSTURE—In playing the bugle, you stand in a natural position, both while practicing and while sounding the calls. Your chest should be out, your shoulders up, your chin drawn back, and your head should be held erect. Hold the bugle with your right hand as shown in figure 2-1. The slide should rest in the heel of your hand to provide support for the instrument. When you are playing, keep your bugle parallel to the deck or tilted up slightly. Slouching or pointing the bugle at the deck in front of you will prevent proper breathing. Aside from the fact that you are a military man and expected to perform your duties in a military manner, you will be able to play the calls properly only if you have the proper posture.

Figure 2-1. - Sounding the bugle.

PLACEMENT OF MOUTHPIECE—Place the mouthpiece firmly, but not tightly, against the center of your lips. The exact placement depends upon the shape of your teeth and your lips. The most comfortable and natural position is the best position for you. However, after you have made your selection of the best place to put the mouthpiece, you should always practice and sound the calls with it in this position.

Your lips should meet inside the mouthpiece, but they must not be clamped together rigidly. They should be free to vibrate since the lips are to the bugle what your vocal chords are to your voice.

You will find that your lips will not vibrate properly unless they are moist. While you are playing, do not dry either your lips or your mouthpiece. If necessary, shake the excess saliva out of the mouthpiece and bugle, but remember—keep your lips and mouthpiece moistened while you are practicing or sounding a call.

The vibrations of your lips and the flow of air which passes through the lips cause the air column within the bugle to vibrate. Remember that it is vibrations which make sound. If you have any doubts as to the importance of your lips in producing a tone, try putting the mouthpiece into your mouth and blowing. You can blow all day and get nothing but the sound of wind for your efforts.

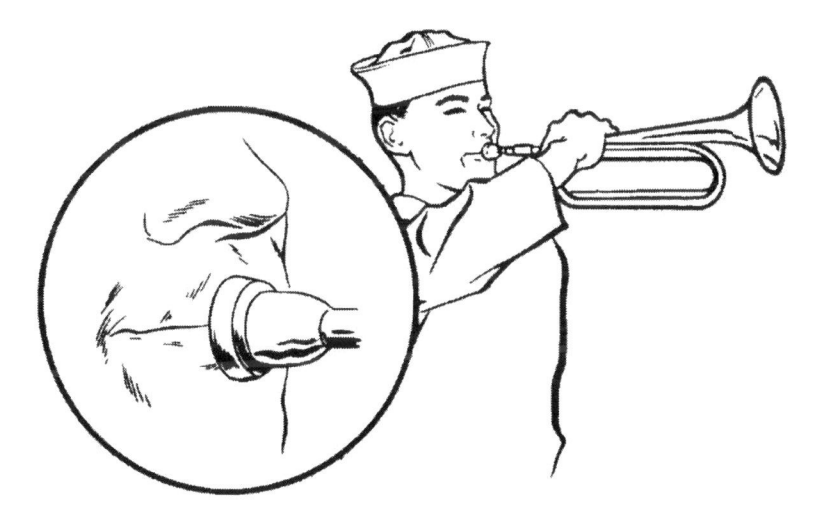

Figure 2-2. - Placement of the mouthpiece.

BREATHING--The importance of proper breathing cannot be over-emphasized. A steam engine will not run without steam under pressure; neither can you sound your calls without a sufficient supply of air. In addition, you are going to have to control this supply of air, just as the steam engine is designed to control its supply of steam in order to accomplish its work.

Some of the ways by which you draw in your supply of air and control it may not seem natural to you, but they have been found necessary by all skillful performers on the bugle and similar instruments. The first step is, of course, drawing the air into your lungs. You do this by breathing in through the corners of your mouth when the mouthpiece is in place. You breathe through your mouth because you cannot draw air in rapidly enough through your nose when you are sounding a long or a fast call.

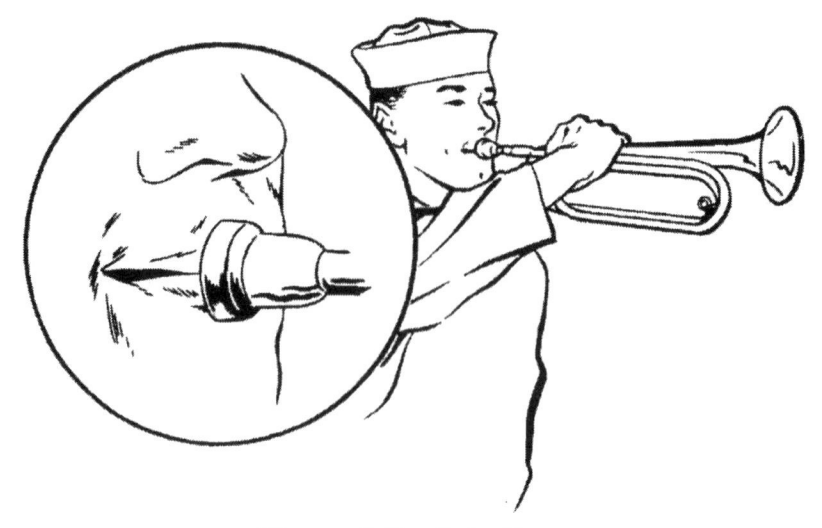

Figure 2-3. - Inhaling.

Storing and controlling your air supply is going to seem just as strange to you as breathing through your mouth; however, if you will follow the steps shown in the illustrations and the discussion beneath them you should have no trouble. The trick is to practice this method of breath control until it becomes natural--that is, until you do not have to think about it.

The most important parts of your breathing apparatus are the lungs, and the diaphragm. The lungs are spongy organs which fill up most of your chest space. Lungs have no muscles, but being elastic, they expand or contract to fill up the space in your chest cavity as it is expanded or contracted. Normally, we think of chest expansion as being outward, and we speak of a chest measurement of --let's say--36 inches, expandable to 39 inches, as being the only possible chest expansion.

However, your chest cavity also expands upward and downward. The upward expansion is taken care of when you stand upright with your head and shoulders back. The expansion downward is the action which is going to concern us here, since it is the part of breathing which is least understood, and the most important to the Bugler.

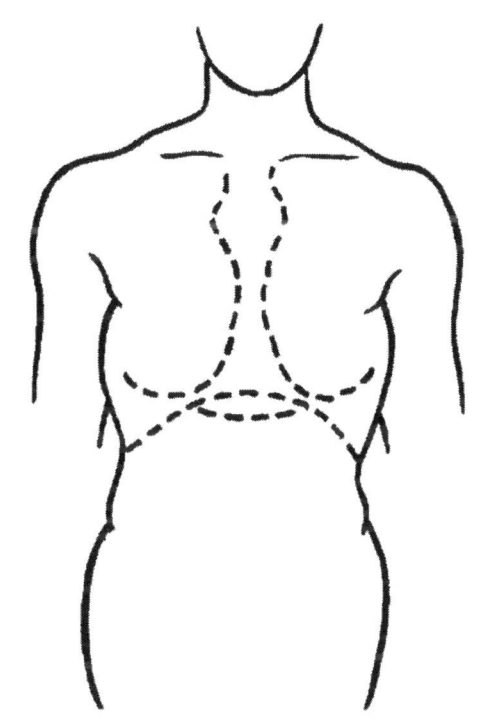

Figure 2-4. - The diaphragm and lungs.

This downward expansion is normally controlled by the diaphragm. The diaphragm is a strong, broad muscle wall which separates the chest cavity from the abdominal cavity. When this muscle is at rest it is shaped as you see in figure 2-4, with its ends lower than the center section.

When you are ready to breathe in, the diaphragm (remember, it is a muscle) contracts and the center section moves down. This increases your chest space. Your lungs expand, a vacuum is crated, and air rushes in to fill this vacuum.

Most people, in their regular breathing, do not make a big enough vacuum and consequently do not draw in enough air. For every-day activity, this does not matter too much, but when they are taking some strenuous exercise, or when they are playing an instrument, their lungs and their diaphragm are not sufficiently well developed to handle the situation. Not only that--they don't know how to go about improving themselves.

The secret lies in making plenty of room for your lungs when you are inhaling. Remember that your lungs are elastic, but have no muscles of their own, and so they will expand just enough to fill the available space.

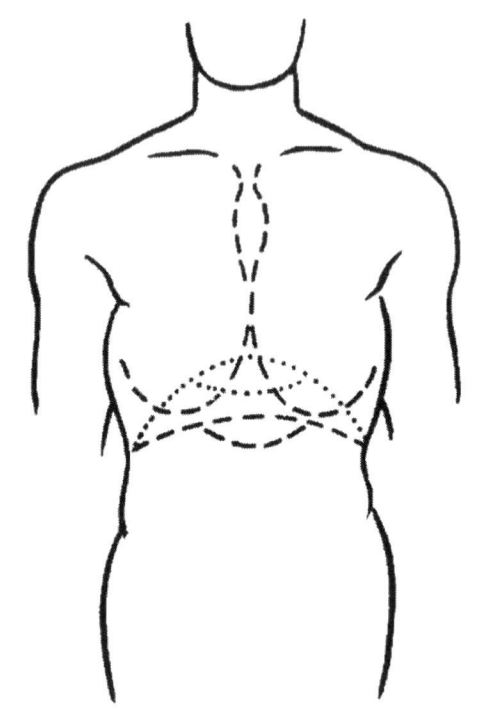

Figure 2-5. - Contraction of the diaphragm.

How do you make this space available? Well, we've already mentioned posture; stand straight, get your shoulders up and back. You have also learned, previously, that the diaphragm flattens out when you breathe, thus making more room for your lungs. It probably occurred to you, then, that the space below the diaphragm isn't exactly a vacuum, and that something has to "give" when the diaphragm moves down.

In our normal breathing we don't give any help to the diaphragm when it compresses the organs beneath it. But, in playing your instrument, YOU MUST RELAX YOUR ABDOMINAL MUSCLES WHEN YOU INHALE. This allows the diaphragm to move down farther, thus making a larger cavity in which the lungs can expand.

In relaxing your abdominal muscles and moving the diaphragm down, you may get the feeling that you are actually pushing out with these muscles. Muscles, like rubber bands, do not push, but pull. It is the diaphragm pulling down that gives you the feeling of pushing. However, the muscular action and the feeling you get are not so important as the fact that your abdomen must move out to make room for more air (see figure 2-6).

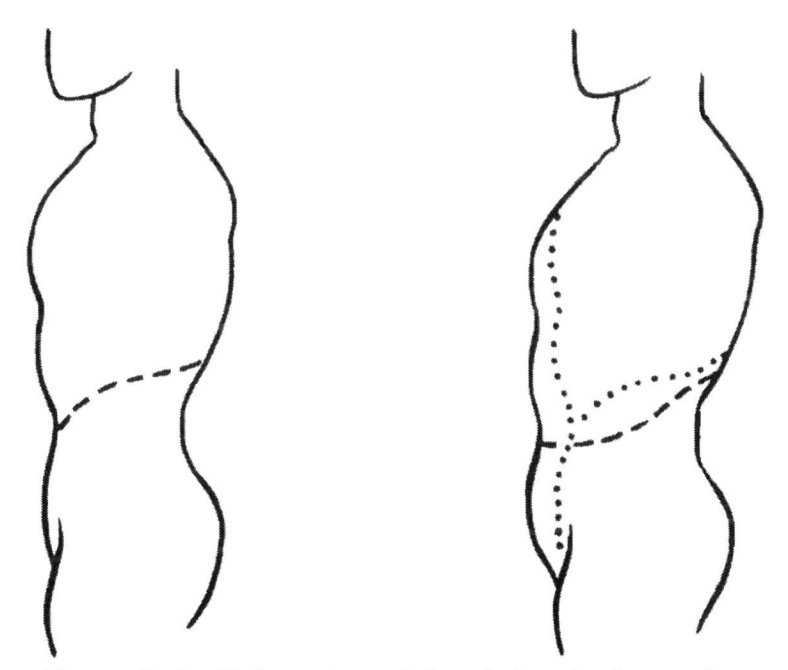

Figure 2-6. - Relaxation of the abdominal muscles.

So far we've talked only about drawing the air in. What happens when you want to sound your bugle? We've mentioned breath control before--here's how you get it.

Instead of squeezing the air out of your chest by contraction of the muscles between your ribs as normally do, put the pressure on from below. Those relaxed abdominal muscles should be tightened as fast or as slowly as is necessary to provide the proper flow of air. Keep a steady pressure on your air supply. Your tongue is the valve which controls the air flow.

A word of caution here: You have probably seen, at some time or other, a Bugler or trumpet player whose cheeks bulged in his efforts to play loud and strong. Puffy cheeks are not necessary; they look ridiculous, and at their worst are quite painful. In addition, you will not have effective lip control if you allow your cheeks to swell.

The action of the tongue in starting and stopping the flow of air is know as TONGUING. After you have drawn in your air supply, the tip of your tongue should touch the base of your upper teeth. Start to pronounce the syllable "ta" and your tongue will, automatically, be in the right place.

Now, with just the mouthpiece in place on your lips and with a comfortable lip tension, say "ta." This action--that is, drawing the tongue back and permitting the air flow to start the sound--is known as the ATTACK.

For a proper attack, the note should start "all at once." You will get this result provided you are careful to place your tongue in a position to say "ta," build up air pressure by tightening your abdominal muscles, and then release the air flow by saying "ta." YOU WILL NOT HAVE A PROPER ATTACK IF YOU "CREEP" INTO THE NOTE BY STARTING THE AIR FLOW WITHOUT FIRST STOPPING IT WITH YOUR TONGUE. Until you have exhausted your air supply, hold your tongue back from your teeth. Keep the air flowing by the pressure of your abdominal muscles. For the time being, keep just enough tension in your lip muscles to prevent air from escaping through your lips outside of the mouthpiece.

Your lips should vibrate so that you get a buzz like the sound of a hornet or a bumblebee from the mouthpiece when it is not in the bugle. Hold the same note for as long as you can. Don't let the tone quaver. In time you should be able to hold a note for more than a minute without any "wobble" in the tone. This will mean that you are developing an embouchure. This French word (pronounced awn' bo sure) is used to refer to the coordination of the muscles in your lips, your face, and your tongue when they're producing a musical note. For the present, the best way to develop an embouchure and improve your breath control is to hold each note as long as you possibly can.

At first, your lips and the corners of your mouth will tire quickly. Stop practicing for a short time when this happens, because if the muscles in your lips and face are tired, you have little control over them, and hence your practice will do you no good.

Keep in mind that your syllable is "ta," and not "tha." The "tha" sound will give you a mushy attack and will, later on, make it impossible for you to play notes rapidly.

To vary your practice, try pinching your lips together slightly. This should give you a higher note than you have had. By pinching your lips together you are increasing the speed of vibration in the lips and therefore the speed of the vibration of the column of air inside the bugle. Avoid increasing the pressure of the mouthpiece against your lips. The added pressure might help you to raise the tone, but it will also cut off the blood circulation in your lips and cause them to tire more quickly. For high tones, push the lower lip out slightly, so as to blow toward the top of the mouth piece.

Summary

In this chapter you have learned that:

1. An upright posture, with the head high and the shoulders back, is necessary to the Bugler.
2. The bugle is held in the right hand with the slide resting in the heel of your palm.
3. The mouthpiece should be placed in the "natural" center of your lips.
4. Your lips are closed within the mouthpiece but with just sufficient tension to permit them to vibrate freely.
5. The lips should be kept moist.
6. You breathe through the corners of your mouth when playing.

7. Your abdominal muscles must be relaxed when you inhale and then tightened slowly to provide the proper column of air for sounding your bugle.
8. The proper attack is made by pronouncing "ta."
9. It is best to practice sustained tones to strengthen your lips and to develop proper breath control.
10. Frequent and short practices are better, at first, than a single long practice period during the day because the muscles in the face and lips tire quickly, just as any seldom used muscle will tire when exercise is first begun.

Chapter Three - Reading Music

All sound is produced by vibrations. Some vibrations are too fast for your ears to hear, but we are only going to worry about those you can hear. Regular vibrations form a musical sound called tone; irregular vibrations make noise.

Very rapid vibrations cause high notes while low notes result from slower vibrations. Musicians refer to the number of vibrations per second, or more specifically to the sound made by a certain number of vibrations per second, as the pitch of a note. For instance, the first note you play on your bugle will quite likely be G with 293 2/3 vibrations per second. (You won't be able to count these, by the way.)

The length of time you hold a note is the duration of that note. Music is made by putting tones of different pitch and duration together.

It's as simple as that, but unless you have an instructor who knows all of the bugle calls used in the Navy, and who can teach them to you, you are going to have to learn to read music before you can put these tones together properly. It isn't as difficult as it may seem.

Musicians use musical notation to indicate the PITCH and DURATION of the notes used in forming the melody. They start with the STAFF which has five regularly spaced lines.

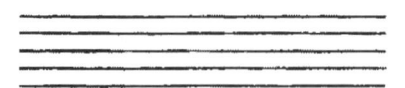

Figure 3-1. - The Staff.

Each line and each space represents a particular pitch for a tone. Then they add the CLEF sign, which will be the "G" or TREBLE CLEF for all bugle music.

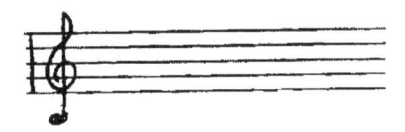

Figure 3-2. - The "G" clef on the Staff.

The notes which are indicated on the staff have been given letter names for ease in referring to them. A series of notes such as shown here is a SCALE.

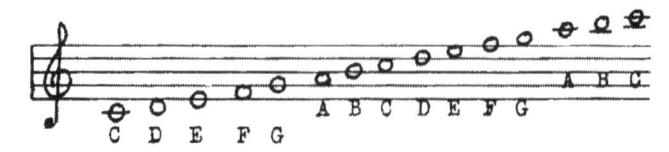

Figure 3-3. - The position of the note on the staff indicates the pitch of the note.

Notice that only the letters A through G are used and that they are repeated several times. Each sequence of notes from A through A, or from B through B, or from G through G, etc., is one OCTAVE.

Notice also that there are notes above and below the staff, and each has its own separate line. These lines are called LEGER LINES. They are continuations of the staff, and they and the spaces between the lines are lettered in the same way as the lines and spaces on the staff.

Your bugle does not play all of these notes however. The staff below shows all of the notes you'll use in your bugle calls.

Figure 3-4. - The bugle sounds these notes. (C, G, C, E, G, B-Flat, C).

The high C is seldom used in bugle calls and the high B-flat is found only in a few drum and bugle corps marches. The flat sign (b) indicates that the pitch of the note which follows it is one-half tone lower than it would otherwise be. Don't worry about how to produce this flatted note. If your instrument is in tune you'll hit it because the bugle was designed to do the job. In fact, you may hit it when you are trying for the high C.

Notes of the same pitch as those found on the bugle would be written for the piano as show below in figure 3-5. The piano notes are indicated by the solid black signs, while the corresponding bugle note is shown by the unshaded symbols. If a piano is available to you, play the notes which are shown in black, so that you can hear the tones which you will use on the bugle.

Figure 3-5. - Piano-bugle note comparison.

So far we have talked about only the pitch of the notes. This is only half of the story. Our musical notation system also indicates the duration, or to be more correct, the RELATIVE DURATION of the notes. Relative duration, or TIME VALUE, of a note is indicated by the same sign which shows you the pitch. (Remember that the location of the sign on the staff shows you the pitch.) Time values of notes are shown by the color (either shaded or unshaded), and by using STEMS and FLAGS, as you can see in the examples below. In some of the examples further on in the chapter you will find that the stems may point either up or down. The direction in which the stem points does not affect the time value of a note. Usually (but not always) the stems point up for notes below the third line of the staff and down for the notes above the third line. Notes on the third line may point in either direction.

The signs for these relative note values are shown in the table below.

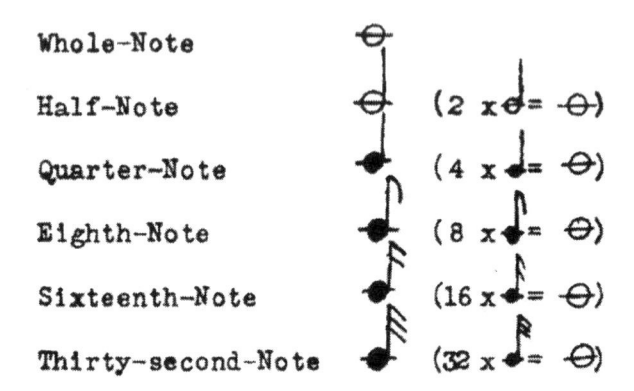

Whole-Note	𝅝	
Half-Note	𝅗𝅥	(2 x 𝅗𝅥 = 𝅝)
Quarter-Note	𝅘𝅥	(4 x 𝅘𝅥 = 𝅝)
Eighth-Note	𝅘𝅥𝅮	(8 x 𝅘𝅥𝅮 = 𝅝)
Sixteenth-Note	𝅘𝅥𝅯	(16 x 𝅘𝅥𝅯 = 𝅝)
Thirty-second-Note	𝅘𝅥𝅰	(32 x 𝅘𝅥𝅰 = 𝅝)

Figure 3-6. - Relative note value is shown by shading, stems, and flags.

The note signs indicate RELATIVE DURATION because—as you can see—they show only that a whole note lasts twice as long as a half note; a half note is held twice as long as a quarter note; and so on. The note signs do not show how many seconds or parts of a second you are to hold any of the notes. A way by which you can find the EXACT duration of a note is discussed later in the chapter. For the present we are interested only in the relationship of these notes to each other.

Which music is written, it is divided into MEASURES, or BARS, as they are sometimes called. The name bar comes from the way in which the measures are indicated.

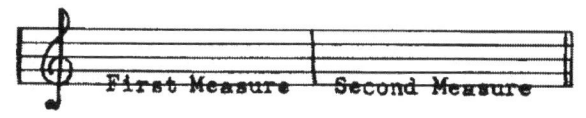

Figure 3-7. - The division line between measures is known as a bar.

(A double-bar, such as you see in the example above, indicates the end of a passage of music. Later on, you will find that a single call may have more than one passage. A new passage generally introduces a new melody or a new rhythm).

Each measure in any passage of music has a definite number of BEATS, or COUNTS. Each of these beats has the same time value, just as the ticks of a clock are always evenly spaced and of the same duration. You have often heard the bass drummer in a military band or a dance orchestra making the beat for his mates or for the dancers. You must have noticed then that the beats were always evenly spaced, no matter how many, or how few notes the other instruments in the band played between beats.

How many beats for a measure? What note has one beat? How long is a beat? For the time being, we will consider only the first two of these questions. The TIME SIGNATURE is used to show the number of beats per measure and the note which has the value of one beat. The time signature is expressed as a fraction as in the sample below. The upper figure in the fraction indicates the number of beats per measure while the lower figure shows the kind of a note which has one beat.

Figure 3-8. - The time signature appears in the first measure of a musical passage.

So, in the illustration above, each measure gets two beats and a quarter-note gets one beat. The other time signatures commonly found in music for the bugle are:

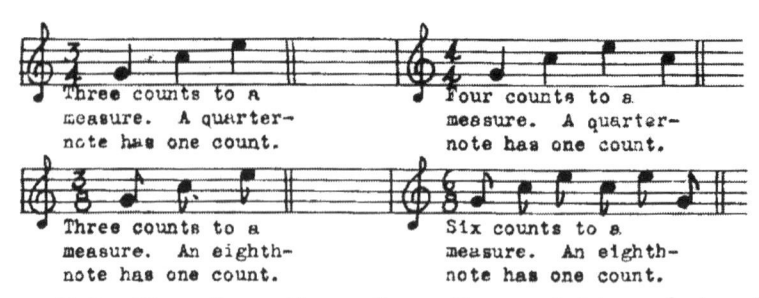

Three counts to a measure. A quarter-note has one count.

Four counts to a measure. A quarter-note has one count.

Three counts to a measure. An eighth-note has one count.

Six counts to a measure. An eighth-note has one count.

Figure 3-9. - Two-four, three-four, three-eight, and six-eight are the time signatures which you will find most often in music for the bugle.

4/4 time is also known as COMMON TIME and a C frequently replaces the fraction.

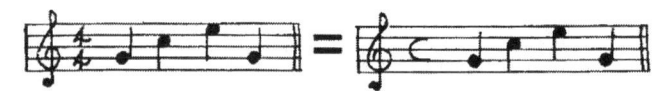

Figure 3-10. - Common time is the most frequently used time signature in music for the bugle.

Remember that in ¾ time it is the quarter-note which gets one beat, while in 3/8 time the eighth-note gets one beat.

In the examples given above, we have used only the notes which have a duration of one beat under the particular time signature, but of course, a measure may have notes which have more than a single beat or it may have a number of notes which get one-half or even a quarter of a beat. For example:

Figure 3-11. - The beats fall as indicated by the arrows above the staff.

In this example in 4/4 time, the quarter-note has the first beat, the four sixteenth-notes fall on the second beat, and the half note is held for the third and fourth beats.

Up to the present we have had our Bugler playing full time, but he does pause occasionally. These pauses are indicated by signs called RESTS. The rests last for the same length of time as the notes which they replace.

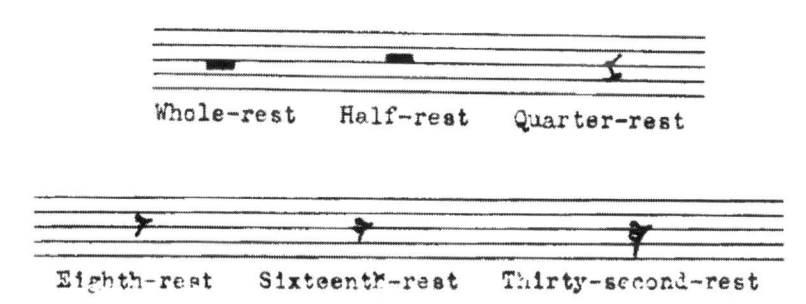

Figure 3-12. - Rests have the same time value as the corresponding notes.

Another sign or symbol which is frequently used is the TIE. This is the curved line shown in the example below. This sign ties the notes so that they are played as a single continuous sound. The tie is used only for notes of the same pitch.

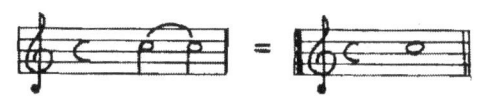

Figure 3-13. - The tie makes a single note of two or more shorter notes.

If notes of different pitch have the curved line over them, or beneath them, this line is called a SLUR. When you play slurred notes you glide from one to the other without interrupting the sound.

Figure 3-14. - The slur indicates that you are to attack only the first note in the series of notes over which it spreads.

Frequently you will see eighth-notes, sixteenth-notes, or thirty-second notes written with a straight line connecting the stems as in the following examples.

Figure 3-15. - Notes are grouped by lines connecting the stems.

These lines are used to replace the individual flags as shown in the examples below.

Figure 3-16. - Usually noted are grouped to form one complete beat.

The straight lines do not change the time values of the notes or the way in which they are played, but are used to make it easier to read the music rapidly. Usually a group of notes connected in this way has one beat.

In order to add to the duration of a note or rest without adding another NOTE or REST sign, a DOT is used.

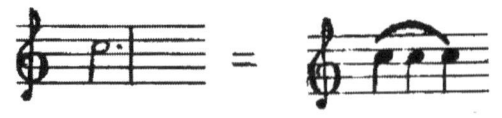

Figure 3-17. - The dot gives the half-note the same time value as three quarter notes would have.

When you see this dot following one of these musical signs, you increase the length of the note or rest by one-half of its previous length. In the first example above we have a dotted half-note. In playing this note you hold it for the same length of time as an ordinary half-note plus a quarter-note, but there is only one continuous sound for the three beats.

Figure 3-18. - In three-four and four-four time, give three beats to a dotted half-note.

Remember that the dot does not add any particular number of beats or parts of a beat, but increases, by one-half, the value of the note which follows. For instance, in the following example of 6/8 time the quarter-note has two beats, the two eighth-notes have one beat each, the dotted eighth-note gets a beat and a half, and the sixteenth-note gets one-half of a beat.

Figure 3-19. - The dot has no specific time value but increases the value of the note before it by one-half.

Here's a different example in 6/8 time:

Figure 3-20. - In this case, the dot adds two beats to the four normally given to a half-note in six-eight time.

Notice that in 6/8 time it is the dotted half-note which gets the full six counts of a measure. Why is this? Well, if an eighth-note gets one beat and a quarter-note gets two, a half-note would have four, and a dotted note would have six counts.

Let's add a few complications. Suppose you have a bar of music as shown in figure 3-21:

Figure 3-21.

You have common time with a dotted quarter-note, three eighth-notes, and a quarter-note in the first measure. This would be played as shown in figure 3-22.

Figure 3-22.

The beats in the measure would fall as indicated by the arrows on the top line of the staff. The dotted quarter-note would get one and one-half counts. Each of the eighth-notes would get one-half count, and the quarter-note, one count.

Another symbol which you'll meet early in your career as a Bugler is the HOLD, or PAUSE, which is a short curved line with a dot beneath it—both placed over a note. The HOLD (figure 3-23) has no specific time value, but indicates that the note beneath it should be held for more than its normal duration.

Figure 3-23. You do not count a held note.

The length of time you will hold a note marked in this way will depend upon your own judgment. In some cases you may want to hold the note for twice its normal value; in other cases it may last four times as long. If you don't have an opportunity to listen to someone who knows the calls and can show you how long the pauses are held, try to fit the length of the pause into the general style of the call.

Dots are used in still another symbol in music. This symbol is called a REPEAT (figure 3-24) and has two dots, one above the other, in front of a double bar.

The REPEAT sign indicates that the player is to go back to the beginning and play the entire passage again. In a few cases where the composer wants only a part of the music to be repeated, he indicates this by placing a double bar with two

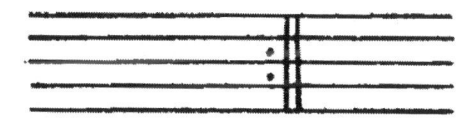

Figure 3-24. - The repeat mark indicates that you are to replay a passage of the music.

dots BEHIND it at the point from which the notes are to be repeated. In such cases you repeat only the music between the reversed repeat sign and the repeat sign.

Figure 3-25. - Notice how much space the use of the repeat mark saves.

The phrase "da capo al fine" (pronounced feenay) which often appears as D.C. al Fine, means "from the beginning to the end." In a repeat like this, the end of the call is indicated by the word "Fine." Turn to Reveille, call No. 86 in chapter 6 and you will see the phrase in use. When you sound Reveille, play all of the music to the "da capo," then go back to the beginning and play to the "Fine." Notice that repeat marks and the da capo are not used interchangeably. With repeat marks you repeat the passage in which the marks are found; with the da capo you repeat the previous passage.

So far, we have talked about note values as though an eighth-note or sixteenth-note always has the same relative duration under any given time signature. That is, in common time, there are eight eighth-notes or sixteen sixteenth notes to the bar with the eighth notes each having one-half of the beat and the sixteenth notes each getting one-quarter of the beat.

You will find an exception to this general rule in some of the calls. Sometimes it is necessary to divide a quarter-note into three eighth-notes instead of just two and quite often an eighth-note is divided into three sixteenth-notes. This division is called a TRIPLET and is indicated by a small figure "3" above or below the grouped notes.

Figure 3-26. - Both sixteenth and eighth-note triplets are shown in this measure.

The group of three sixteenth-notes is played in the same time as would normally be given to two sixteenths. The group of three eighth-notes has the same value as you would usually give to two eighths.

So, in the example above, you will play the first eighth-note and the group of three sixteenth-notes on the first beat while the group of three eighth-notes will be played on the second beat.

Up to this point we have talked about beats or counts as though a beat had only one possible duration. But you know that if you tap your foot to keep time you can tap as fast or as slow as you like. So, the composer of a call needs some way to describe to you his idea of how fast or how slow you should make your counts. The number of beats per minute is known as the TEMPO of the music. One of the faults of many Buglers is that they try to sound the calls too rapidly. This results in a call which sounds like potatoes rolling down the cellar steps.

Sometimes the composer will use words, such as "quick" or "slow" to describe the tempo of a call. He might even use words from a foreign language which mean the same thing such as "allegro" or "largo." But this method still isn't very accurate because your idea of fast or slow may be different from his. However, there is a method of marking which will show you the exact tempo intended by the composer. Above the clef and the time signature of the calls you will find either a quarter-note, a dotted quarter, or an eighth-note with a number beside it. The number tells you how many quarter-notes, dotted quarter-notes or eighth-notes to play in one minute. For example:

Figure 3-27. - The tempo marking ([quarter note]-120) shows you the exact speed at which the music is to be played.

In the example above there are 120 quarter notes to the minute and by referring to the time signature you can see that each quarter note gets one count. (This, by the way, is standard march tempo.)

To get the exact tempo, tap your foot in what you think is a good marching speed, and count the number of taps in fifteen seconds. You should have tapped 30 times during those fifteen seconds. You can keep track of the number of measures by counting 1-2, 2-2, 3-2, 4-2 and so on. In 2/4 time you will, of course, play fifteen measures in the fifteen seconds, if your tempo is [quarter-note] =120.

If you have a dotted quarter-note in the tempo marking, as in the example below, use the same general method to find your tempo.

Figure 3-28. - Six-eight tempos this fast are ordinarily counted as though there were but two beats to the measure.

Here we have 6/8 time with 152 dotted quarters to the minute. This is quite a bit faster than the last example. You are going to tap your foot 152 times in one minute, and a quarter of that or 38 times in fifteen seconds. A dotted quarter-note, as you know is equal to three eighth-notes between each tap. This may seem to be quite a trick, but if you will follow the steps outlined below you should have no trouble.

1. Start tapping your foot.
2. Select the proper tempo by checking with your watch.
3. When you have the tempo, try whistling or playing dotted quarter-notes in time to the beat; then play three eighth notes per beat. Remember the fault we mentioned before, and don't try to play too fast. Keep your notes sharp and clean.

Sometimes you will see the tempo marking indicated in a slightly different way than was give above. For example: M. M. [quarter-note] =120.

The M. M. is an abbreviation for Maelzel's Metronome. Maelzel invented the system for indicating tempo that you have just learned and he also invented the machine called the METRONOME which is often used to measure the beat. This machine is a lot like a clock, but you can set it so that the tick will mark the time for any tempo you want. You set the metronome by moving a small weight up or down the pendulum which is engraved with numbered lines to show the setting for all of the tempos used in music.

The latest metronomes are electrical and are set by moving a pointer to the desired setting.

In addition to the pitch and duration, there is another important bit of information about a note which you can get from music symbols. This information concerns the INTENSITY or VOLUME of a sound, and is shown by words such as "soft" or "loud" and by DYNAMIC MARKS. The CRESENDO (increase) mark < tells you that the volume of tone should be gradually increased. The DECRESENDO (decrease) mark > indicates that the volume should be gradually reduced.

The two marks together <> are known as a SWELL; this sign indicates that the intensity of the tone first increases and then decreases. All of these marks are inserted by the composer to show you the proper length of time for the crescendo and decresendo. A crescendo, for example, may continue for several measures, or it may be marked for a single quarter note.

Dynamic marks do not appear often in music for the bugle, because, since the calls serve as signals, they are written to be played "loud." However, you will find the marks used quite frequently in the exercises in Chapter 5, "Bugle Practice," because practicing swells is excellent for developing breath control.

You have now had an explanation of all of the signs which you will see in the bugle calls for the US Navy, as published in this manual. As a review, try to name each of the signs used in the call below, and tell what each sign indicates.

Name both the pitch and the time value for each note. When you are sure that you understand the meaning of each symbol try beating the rhythm out with your feet. When you have the rhythm, hum or whistle the notes.

You should be able to recognize the call. You probably will not hit the exact pitch of the first note unless you have a piano available. The pitch of the first note does not matter in this exercise so long as you remember to keep the INTERVALS the same. An interval is the distance along the musical scale from one note to another. So, if the music shows that one tone is two steps above another on the musical scale it make little difference in this practice whether you start on a "C" or a "G" provided you keep the two step interval. The "do-re-mi" of your school days should be of great help to you in working this out.

Figure 3-29. - This is a call which you have heard many times. Read the music, identify the symbols, tap out the rhythm, hum the notes, and recognize the call.

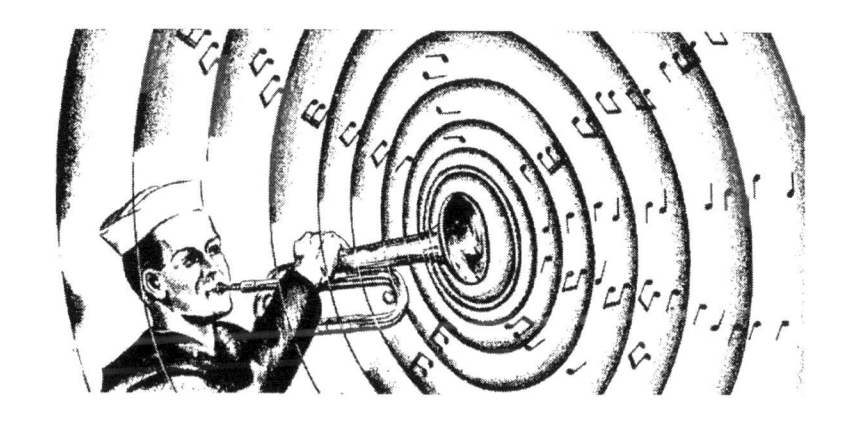

Chapter Four - Starting Your Practice

You are ready now to practice some written exercises designed to develop both your ability to read music and your skill as a Bugler. However, before you start to practice read all of this chapter and take a look at the exercises in chapter 5. Supplement the exercises in chapter 4 with those in chapter 5. The latter chapter has been arranged to show you approximately what your rate of progress should be. If you have had previous experience in reading music or in playing an instrument, you may be able to start practice on the calls before the end of the 15-week period, or, if you are studying without the benefit of even part-time help from an instructor, your progress may be somewhat slower than that given in the schedule.

When you have finished your reading, start with the following exercise. Play it through often enough so that you can attack each note without fumbling and can hold each note for...

...its full value without wavering. Remember to moisten your lips before you begin. Draw a breath after each note the first few times you play this, then take two notes in a single breath, and so on, until you can play the entire exercise without drawing a fresh breath.

If you have no piano available so that you can hear the low C (see chapter 3 for corresponding bugle-piano notes), just remember that this note is the lowest note which can be sounded on the bugle. The G is the next note, while the C above that is the next step on the bugle. When you have had more practice, you will automatically associate the correct note pitch and the proper lip tension for that pitch with each of the written notes.

Do not try to play above the C shown in this exercise until your embouchure and your breath control are well enough developed to play the complete exercise without error.

Breath Control

Here is an exercise which will help you in developing breath control:

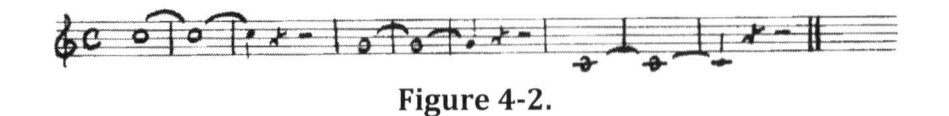

Figure 4-2.

Notice that with a tempo in which a quarter note equals 60, each halfnote has a duration of two seconds. Each of the four notes of the same pitch is tied to the others, so that for each series of notes of the same pitch you will make just one attack. In other words, hold the C, the G, the C again, and the low C, each for seven seconds.

Lip Practice

When you have mastered the first two exercises, practice this one. Remember that your air pressure comes from the tension of your abdominal muscles. The high notes will require slightly more air pressure than the low notes because the opening between your lips is going to be smaller for the high notes.

Practice changing pitch by increasing or decreasing your lip tension without increasing the pressure of the mouthpiece against your lip. Notice that you do not part your lips. You force a column of air through them, and the tension in your lips determines the size of the opening between them.

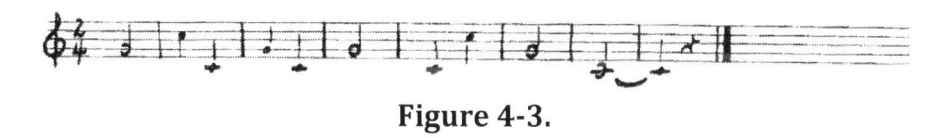

Figure 4-3.

Advanced Lip Practice

Provided your lip is strong enough now to hit and hold the three lower notes on the bugle, you are ready to add the E to your musical vocabulary. Do not try to force the note. The increase in lip tension and air pressure from C to E is very slight. Control over your lip muscles does not come in a day's time.

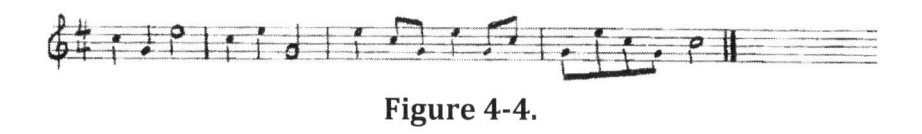

Figure 4-4.

When you can sound the E with no strain or difficulty add the high G. Don't try to go too fast. It is far better to be able to hit the lower notes when and as you want, than to be able to hit all of the notes—once in a while. Your lips require considerable training and strengthening before you can hope to play with ease beyond the three lower notes on the bugle.

Figure 4-5.

You must continue to practice sustained tones on all of the notes as you add new ones. However, as you know or will soon know, sustained high notes are very tiring to your lips. You should, therefore, practice the high notes only as long as the development of your embouchure will permit, because practice with tired lip muscles is more detrimental than beneficial.

Tonguing

Up to this point we have been concerned with the development of your lip and breath control. However, your tongue has an equally important part in sounding bugle calls. In all cases it is your tongue which determines the sharpness of the attack for a note. For a clean, sharp attack, you first build up air pressure by contraction of the abdominal muscles while using your tongue as a valve to prevent the air from escaping. Then, by saying "ta" you start the flow of air instantaneously.

When you release notes of short duration, such as most quarter notes, eighth, and sixteenth notes, stop the air flow by replacing the tip of your tongue at the base of your upper teeth, where it will be ready for the next attack. With considerable practice you should be able to play four clean sixteenth notes to the beat in march tempo [quarter-note] = 120, using the tonguing method previously described, which is known as SINGLE-TONGUING. However, when you are sounding longer note values, such as half and whole notes, or quarter notes in slow tempos, you do not use your tongue to release the note, but stop the flow of air by relaxing the abdominal pressure on your diaphragm.

There are some bugle calls which require greater speed in tonguing than you can manage by single-tonguing. It is necessary, therefore, to use other methods to tongue these very rapid changes.

Triple-Tonguing

The most frequently used method is known as TRIPLE-TONGUING although a very few of the calls require DOUBLE-

TONGUING. The syllables used in triple-tonguing are "ta-ta-ka." Normally, each of the syllables is given exactly the same time value. However, for your early practice, it is wise to put more stress on the "ka" than on the first two syllables, because saying "ka" requires a throat movement which is more difficult than the tongue movement used in saying "ta." You will have to practice this method for tonguing very slowly at first. When you begin it will seem, and will be, slower than single-tonguing. However, eventually you will find that you can play sixteenth note triplets, such as are found in the following call, with ease:

Figure 4-6.

Remember that the ability to sound the calls properly will not be yours automatically. Your tongue needs as much practice to be able to move rapidly and in the right direction as your body would if you were called upon to do flips on a tight wire.

Practice the following exercise carefully, starting very slowly, and gradually speed up your tonguing until you can play it at a tempo of [quarter-note] =132 without error. Make every note distinct.

Figure 4-7.

Double-Tonguing

Double-tonguing is considered by most Buglers, to be more difficult than triple-tonguing. The syllables used are "ta-ka" as is shown in the following exercise. Start slowly, as you did in practicing triple-tonguing, and increase the speed gradually until you can play the exercise in rapid tempo.

Figure 4-8.

When you think that your embouchure has developed to the point that you are ready to sound the high B flat and high C, by all means, do so. You should, however, be able to sound all of the lower notes without error and without having to "work up to them" before you attempt these two top notes. Keep in mind that you should raise note-pitch by increasing lip tension and air pressure rather than by increasing the pressure of the mouthpiece against your lips.

The most important thing that you should have learned from this chapter is that you can become a good Bugler only by constant and intelligent practice. Unfortunately, there are no short cuts or tricks to be used as substitutes for proper technique. This practice should gradually develop your coordination in breathing, lip tension, and tonguing to the point where you sound all of the calls perfectly.

Additional exercises are included in the next chapter. These exercises range from very simple to very difficult. Unless you have an instructor to check on your progress and arrange your practice program for you, it is suggested that you follow the schedule of exercises as shown. This schedule is based on an assumption that you will be able to practice at least eight hours every week.

Chapter Five - Bugle Practice

The exercises in this chapter are arranged in order of difficulty to enable you to progress smoothly from beginner to bugle player. It is expected that you will be able to practice at least eight hours a week. Your practice room should be located in an area in which you will not be interrupted too frequently and, if possible, where the calls which you are practicing will not be mistaken for the real thing.

You will not be expected to become an accomplished performer in 15 weeks of practice, of course, but during this period you should gain enough skill on the bugle to enable you to work out unfamiliar calls without the aid of an instructor.

Tempo markings have not been placed on the exercises in this chapter because it is expected that the tempo will vary as you gain proficiency.

Bugle Exercises

FIRST WEEK.—During your first week of practice, concentrate on sounding a full, clear tone on the bugle. Remember to moisten your lips before you begin.

Exercise 1.

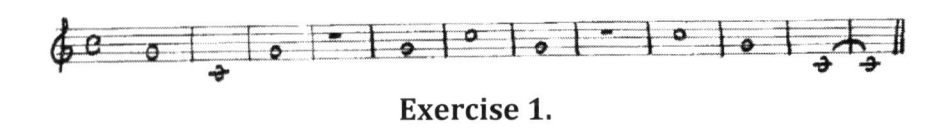

Exercise 2.

Exercise 3.

SECOND WEEK.—When you practice the E in the exercises for the second week, reach the note by increasing your lip tension and air pressure rather than by increasing the pressure of the mouthpiece against your lips.

Exercise 4.

Exercise 5.

Exercise 6.

THIRD WEEK.—Practice the long tones in exercise No. 7 only for as long as the development of embouchure will permit. When your lip commences to tire put your bugle aside for a moment. When you play the slurred tones in exercise No. 9, remember that you play both notes without stopping the flow of air.

FOURTH WEEK.—You will find that it is more difficult to play slurred notes when you are going up than when you are going down; however, you should be able to do both with ease.

FIFTH WEEK.—Exercise No. 13 is intended to give you practice in rhythm. Practice it first at [quarter-note] = 120; then take it at [quarter-note] = 180. In exercise No. 14, give each quarter note one full count; give the eighth notes one-half count, give full value to the eighth rests.

Exercise 13.

Exercise 14.

Exercise 15.

SIXTH WEEK.—In exercise No. 18, give a full six counts to the dotted half notes.

Exercise 16.

Exercise 17.

Exercise 18.

SEVENTH WEEK.—Do not strain to reach the G in these long tone exercises. If the muscles of your lips are ready you will be able to sound it without difficulty.

Exercise 19.

Exercise 20.

Exercise 21.

EIGHTH WEEK.—Observe the swells in exercise No. 22. Start the exercise softly, increase the volume gradually to very loud, and then diminish the volume slowly to soft. Exercise No. 23 is the second half of a call with which you are familiar. Exercise No. 24 has a tricky rhythm with a dotted eighth note and a sixteenth note following two eighth notes. Practice this exercise very slowly until you give the proper time value to both eighth notes and dotted eighth note in the same measure.

Exercise 22.

Exercise 23.

Exercise 24.

NINTH WEEK.—Exercise No. 25 will give you further practice in slurring. Exercise No. 26 is a call with which you may be familiar. Play the call through slowly at first to learn the note pitch. Then, sound it at a tempo of [quarter-note] = 132. In exercise No. 27 you must keep a strict count of three for each measure. Double-tongue the sixteenth notes.

TENTH WEEK.—Exercises No. 28, 29 and 30 give you further practice in double-tonguing.

ELEVENTH WEEK.—In exercise No. 31 you have additional practice in sounding dotted eighth notes and sixteenth notes. Exercise No. 32 is a call which is certainly familiar to you. It should be sounded at a very slow tempo.

Exercise 31.

Exercise 32.

Exercise 33.

TWELFTH WEEK.—Exercise No. 34 is the first passage of a well-known bugle call. Exercise No. 36 is another familiar call.

Exercise 34.

Exercise 35.

Exercise 36.

THIRTEENTH WEEK.—Exercise No. 37 has been included to give you practice in rapid changing of your embouchure. Practice the exercise slowly at first. Exercise No. 38 is another call which you will recognize. The triplets in exercise No. 39 should be triple-tongued.

Exercise 37.

Exercise 38.

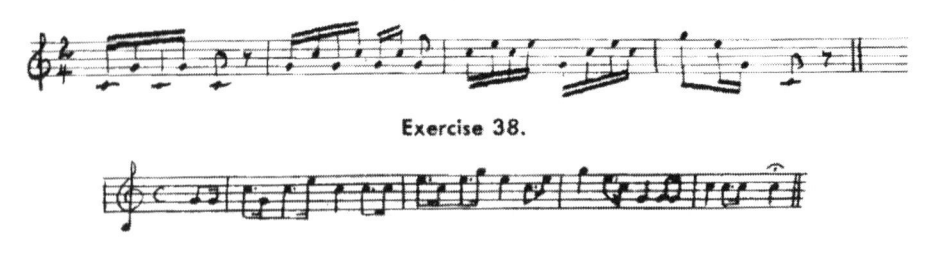

Exercise 39.

FOURTEENTH WEEK.—Continue your work on triple-tonguing in exercise No. 40. Exercise No. 41 introduces one of the most difficult of the calls insofar as tempo is concerned because it includes both eighth and sixteenth note triplets. You will have to count this one very carefully in order to give the proper time value to the notes, particularly in the third and seventh full measures. Exercise No. 42 adds the high C to your note-pitch vocabulary. Do not mistake the high B-flat for the C. Remember that the high C is exactly one octave above the C which starts the exercise.

Exercise 40.

Exercise 41.

Exercise 42.

FIFTEENTH WEEK.—Exercise No. 43 gives you the complete range of the bugle scale. Practice this exercise, observing the dynamic markings closely.

Exercise No. 44 is written with intervals of an octave to give you practice in breath control and lip tension.

Exercise 43.

Exercise 44.

Exercise 45.

When you can play exercise No. 45 without error you are ready to start practicing on the calls.

Chapter Six - The Calls

This chapter contains all of the bugle calls in use in the United States Navy. The calls have been classified only as ROUTINE, EMERGENCY, or ROUTINE AND EMERGENCY in order to clarify previous classifications. The calls have been placed in alphabetical order to facilitate location.

The musical signs and symbols used are those which have been explained in previous chapters, with the exception of the ⊢⊣. This symbol is a rest or pause of indefinite duration which appears in calls used during marches or drills. Where the pause appears in a call, the preparatory command may be given at any appropriate time prior to the execution of the movement, but the command of execution is to be given when the body of troops has reached the point where execution of the movement is to be made. The command of execution is given on the right foot for movements to the right and on the left foot for movements to the left.

It would be wise for you to consult your Chief as to which of the calls are used most frequently on board your ship so that you can learn these calls first. Of course, this does not relieve you of the responsibility of learning the other calls, particularly the emergency calls, but it will permit you to "bear down" on those most useful to you. All of the calls must be played from memory exactly as they are written. This will necessitate considerable practice on each call in order to commit all the calls to memory with the correct tune and tempo. The practice should be done in an assigned space below decks to avoid the confusion which might result if, for example, Liberty Call were to be sounded at sea.

1. Abandon Ship.—Emergency—sounded as a signal to man boats and abandon ship.

2. Adjutant's Call.—Routine—at shore stations sounded as a signal for companies to form battalion. Immediately after call, the adjutant posts the guides of the color company and this company marches in line.

Used on board ship in special ceremonies. (See Taps.)

3. Admiral's Barge.—Routine—sounded as a signal to call away the admiral's barge. It may also be used to call away any barge. The particular barge desired is designated by C-note blasts.

4. Aircraft Elevators.—Routine—sounded to call away aircraft elevators. If necessary, C-note blasts can be used to designate the particular elevator and elevator pump room to be manned. The call is identical to the Wherry call.

5. Assembly.—Routine—sounded as a signal for assembly of details or companies at a designated place. This call is identical to division.

6. As Skirmishers, March.—Routine—although this call is generally used in connection with maneuvering troops in the field, it is frequently used aboard ship as a call to deploy for physical drill.

7. Attention.—Routine —sounded as a signal for all hands to stand at attention and maintain silence. When sounded for passing honors, it is a positive command for every man in sight from the outboard to stand at attention and face the passing vessel.

8. Attention to orders.—Routine—sounded as a signal that important information is to be passed. Demands silence but does not require the position of attention.

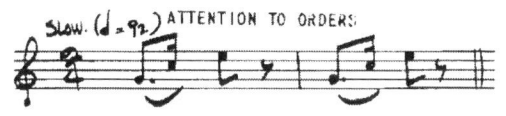

9. Automobile Call.—Routine—sounded to call away a motor vehicle. The particular vehicle desired can be designated by E-notes blasts.

10. Band Call.—Routine—sounded as a signal to call the band to quarterdeck or any other previously designated position. It is most frequently heard following Full Guard or Guard of the Day when colors are being saluted or honors presented.

11. Bear A Hand.—Routine—sounded as a signal to indicate haste in obeying a previous order or call.

Quick (♩.=176)   BEAR A HAND

[musical notation]

12. Belay.—Routine—sounded as a signal to countermand or revoke a previous call or order. If necessary, the previous call should be repeated, followed immediately by Belay.

(♩=132)   BELAY

[musical notation]

13. By the Left Flank, March.—Routine—the four descending notes are the preparatory command for the movement to the left flank. The G-note blast is the command of execution and should be given as the left foot strikes the ground when the body of troops has reached the point where execution of the movement is to be made.

(♩=132)   BY THE LEFT FLANK, MARCH

[musical notation — Column proceeds to flanking point]

14. By the Right Flank, March.—Routine—the four ascending notes are the preparatory command for the movement to the right flank. The G-note blast is the command of execution and should be given as the right foot strikes the ground when the body of troops has reached the point where execution of the movement is to be made.

(♩=132)   BY THE RIGHT FLANK, MARCH

[musical notation — Column proceeds to flanking point]

15. Call All Signalmen.—Routine—sounded to call the signal gang to muster on the signal bridge.

[Musical notation: Quick ♩=152, "CALL ALL SIGNALMEN"]

16. Call Away All Boats.—Routine—sounded as a signal to call away all boats for exercise or when all boats are to be used for a landing or for an armed boat expedition.

[Musical notation: Quick (♩=200), "CALL AWAY ALL BOATS"]

17. Captain's Gig (Staff Gig).—Routine—sounded as a signal to call away the captain's gig. When more than one gig is in use the particular gig desired may be designated by C-note blasts.

[Musical notation: ♩=138, "CAPTAIN'S GIG (STAFF GIG)"]

18. Carry On.—Routine—sounded after Attention to Orders as a signal to resume activities underway before the interruption.

[Musical notation: (♩=108), "CARRY ON"]

19. Cease Firing.—Routine—sounded as a signal to cease firing or to knock off fueling.

[Musical notation: Quick ♩=152, "CEASE FIRING"]

20. Charge.—Emergency—sounded in the field as a signal for a charge. This call is identical to Man Overboard.

21. Church Call.—Routine—this call signals that divine services are about to be held. Aboard ship the call is followed by the tolling of the ship's bell. The call may also be used to form a funeral escort.

22. Clean Bright Work.—Routine—sounded as a signal to clean assigned bright work or to take up assigned detail work.

23. Column Left, March.—Routine—the first two measures are the preparatory command for the column left movement. The G-note blast is the command of execution and should be given as the left foot strikes the ground when the body of troops has reached the point where execution of the movement is to be made.

24. Column Right, March.—Routine—the first two measures are the preparatory command for the column right movement. The G-note blast is the command of execution and should be given as the right foot strikes the ground when the body of troops has reached the point where execution of the movement is to be made.

25. Commence Firing.—Routine—sounded as a signal to begin firing.

26. Commence Fueling.—Routine—sounded as a signal to begin fueling. This call is identical to Commence Firing.

27. Companies.—Routine—sounded to alert companies of men as units. If it is necessary to alert a single company, this company is designated by G-note blasts.

28. Crash Boat.—Emergency—this call is sounded as signal for the boat crew to man the designated crash boat (designated by C-note blasts if more than one crash boat is aboard). The Hospitalman reports immediately at the boat with his medical kit. The deck division concerned with lowering the boat stands by. The crane operator goes to his station and sees that the power is on and that the crane is ready to operate.

[Musical notation: CRASH BOATS, ♩=132]

29. Cutter.—Routine—sounded as a signal to call away a cutter. The particular cutter desired may be designated by C-note blasts.

[Musical notation: CUTTER, (♩=132)]

30. Dinghy.—Routine—sounded as a signal to call away a dinghy. The particular dinghy desired may be designated by C-note blasts.

[Musical notation: DINGHY, Quick ♩=152]

31. Dismiss.—Routine—sounded after Secure, or sounded alone after drills as a signal to dismiss a division.

[Musical notation: DISMISS, Quick ♩=132]

32. Division.—Routine—sounded as a signal to call a designated division to quarters. It is followed by C-note blasts to designate the division desired. This call is identical to Assembly.

[Musical notation: DIVISION, Quick ♩=200]

33. Double Time, March.—Routine—used when on the march to take up the double time (cadence of 180 paces to the minute.) This call is similar to Bear a Hand.

[Musical notation: ♩. = 66, DOUBLE TIME, MARCH]

34. Drill Call.—Routine—sounded as a warning to turn out for a drill.

[Musical notation: Quick ♩ = 152, DRILL CALL]

35. Evening Colors.—Routine—this call (also known as Retreat) is sounded by the Bugler at sundown each evening during the flag-lowering ceremony at all naval stations, marine barracks, naval or marine camps, and aboard ship.

[Musical notation: Moderato ♩ = 120, EVENING COLORS]

Prior to the beginning of the ceremony, Attention is sounded by the Bugler. After a short pause he sounds Evening Colors. The flag leaves the peak or truck at the first note of the call and is lowered at a speed which will bring it to the arms of the flag guard with the last note of the call. Upon completion of Evening Colors the Bugler sounds Carry On.

When a band is present at the ceremony the procedure described above is followed, except that the flag is lowered while the band plays the national anthem. The national anthem follows Evening Colors in the ceremony and is followed by Carry On sounded on the bugle.

36. Extra Duty Men.—Routine—sounded as a signal for extra duty men to fall in at designated position.

37. Face to the Rear.—Routine—this call is sounded for the About Face or Face the Rear.

38. Fire Call.—Emergency—this call is sounded in case of fire or fire drill as a signal for general assembly. The call is usually followed by one or more blasts, as specified in fire orders, to designate the location of the fire. Aboard ship, the call is sounded simultaneously with the ringing of the ship's bell. One blast indicates that the fire is forward. Two blasts indicate that the fire is aft. The call is repeated as many times as the emergency requires.

39. First Call.---Routine---sounded as a warning signal for roll call formations and for most other ceremonies, except mounting of the guard. It is sounded five minutes before morning and evening colors as a signal for the guard, band, and divisions to assemble.

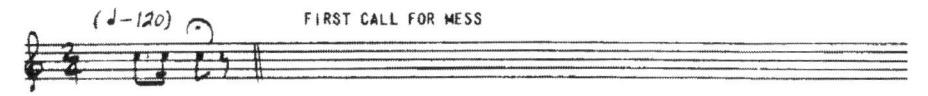

40. First Call for Mess.---Routine---this call may be sounded five minutes before mess call, but is seldom used.

41. Fix Bayonets.—Emergency—used in the field as a signal to fix bayonets. This call is identical to Crash Boats

42. Flag Officer's March.—Routine—upon completion of the last flourish honoring an officer of flag rank, the Bugler may be required to sound the Flag Officer's March. (See Honors.)

43. Flight Quarters.—Routine—sounded as a signal for all aviation crews to go to their stations. C-note blasts can be used to designate type of operations (launching, recovery, respotting, or other) to be undertaken.

44. Forward, March.—Routine—sounded as a signal to begin the march.

45. Full Guard.—Routine—sounded as a signal to call the full bluejacket or Marine guard to the quarterdeck or other designated place.

46. General Muster.—Routine—sounded as a signal for all divisions to assemble for general muster.

47. General Quarters.—**Emergency**—this call is sounded as a signal for all hands to report to their general quarters' station.

48. Go In Water.—**Routine**—sounded after Swimming Call as a signal for the swimming party to go in the water. The life guard boat should be in position and the boom lowered before the call is sounded.

49. Guard of the Day.—**Routine**—sounded as a signal for the assembly of the guard of the day at the quarterdeck or other designated place.

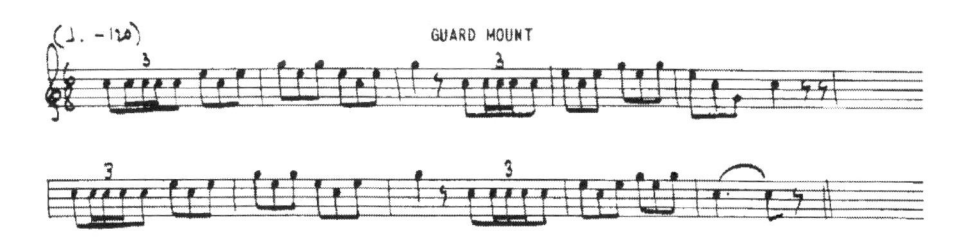

50. Guard Mount.—**Routine**—used in the field to signal that guard mount is about to begin.

51. Guide Center.—**Routine**—sounded on the march as a signal that the guide is to the center.

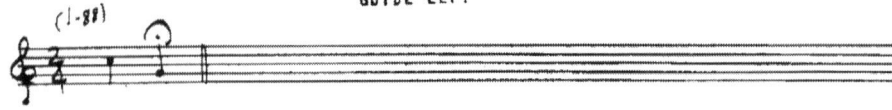

52. Guide Left.—Routine—sounded on the march as a signal that the guide is to the left.

53. Guide Right.—Routine—sounded on the march as a signal that the guide is to the right.

54. Halt.—Routine—sounded on the march as a signal to halt.

55. Hammocks.—Routine—sounded as signal for every man using a hammock to fall in abreast his hammock and maintain silence. Also sounded as signal that bunks may be taken down.

[Sheet music: "HONORS" — ♩=120 — One Flourish; Two Flourishes; Three Flourishes; Four Flourishes]

56. Honors.—Routine—in the absence of a band the Bugler may be required to sound Honors and the Flag Officer's March to salute a visiting dignitary. Honors are rendered by giving the number of flourishes prescribed by Navy Regulations for the rank of the honored official.

The flourish or flourishes are sounded immediately after the visiting official or group of officials has reached the upper platform and saluted the colors. Navy Regulations provide that four flourishes be given to the President of the United States, an ex-President, the Vice President, a member of the President's Cabinet, Under Secretaries and Assistant Secretaries of the Army, Navy, and Air Force, the Chief Justice, ambassadors, the governor of a state or of a territory or possession of the United States, the President pro tempore of the Senate, the Speaker of the House of Representatives, Congressional committees, admirals and generals of four star rank or above, and personages of similar rank from a foreign government, including members of a reigning royal family.

Three flourishes are sounded for envoys extraordinary, vice admirals, and lieutenant generals of the United States, and officials of foreign governments holding similar ranks.

Two flourishes are sounded for ministers resident or diplomatic representatives, rear admirals, and major generals of the United States, and for officials of foreign countries holding similar ranks.

One flourish is sounded for Charge d'affaires, consul generals, commodores, and brigadier generals of the United States, and officials of foreign governments holding similar ranks.

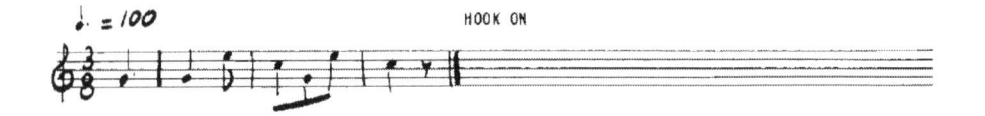

57. Hook On.—Routine—sounded as a signal to hook on and prepare for hoisting the boat or boats whose call has preceded the hook-on signal.

58. Inspection.—Routine—sounded as a signal to prepare for the commanding officer's inspection of personnel, ship, or station.

59. Knock Off Bright Work.—Routine—sounded as a signal to stow all cleaning gear.

60. Knock Off Fueling.—Routine—sounded as a signal to cease fueling. This call is identical to Cease Firing.

61. Left Oblique, March.—**Routine**—the first three notes are the preparatory command for a left oblique movement. The C-note blast is the command of execution and should be given as the left foot strikes the ground when the body of troops has reached the point where execution of the movement is to be made.

62. Liberty Party.—**Routine**—sounded as a signal for the liberty party to fall in for inspection.

63. Lie Down.—**Routine**—sounded in the field as a signal to fall out and rest.

64. Light Smoking Lamp.—**Routine**—this call signals permission for the crew to smoke.

65. Mail Call.—**Routine**—sounded as a signal that mail is ready for distribution.

66. Main Battery Fire Control Exercise.—Routine—sounded as a signal before an exercise for all elements of the main battery fire-control system.

67. Man AA Machine Gun Battery.—Routine and emergency—sounded as a signal to man the AA machine gun battery for drill or other purposes.

68. Man Overboard.—Emergency—this call is used as a signal that there is a man overboard. When the call is sounded, the lifeboat crew mans and lowers its boat, and the lifebuoy guard tosses a buoy into the water as close as possible to the man.

69. Man Radars.—Routine and emergency—sounded as a signal for radar crews to man their stations. If necessary, individual units can be designated by C-note blasts.

70. Man Range Finder.—**Routine**—this call, without designating notes, is a signal to man all range finders. Individuals range finders may be called into action by using an established number of C-note blasts after the call to indicate the proper instrument and crew.

71. Man Search Lights.—**Routine and emergency**—this call, without designating notes, is a signal to man all searchlights. Individual searchlights may be called into action by using an established number of C-note blasts after the call to indicate the proper searchlight and crew.

72. Man the Boat Falls.—**Routine**—a signal for all hand to man the boat falls which are indicated either orally or by boat call.

73. Man Torpedo Defense Battery.—Routine and emergency—sounded as a signal for torpedo defense crews to go to their stations.

74. Mess Call.—Routine—sounded as a signal for crew to assemble for breakfast, dinner, or supper. Also used as a signal for mess cooks to spread mess gear.

75. Morning Colors.—Routine—this call is sounded by the Bugler during flag raising at 0800 each morning at all naval stations, Marine barracks, camps, and aboard ship.

The flag begins to ascent at the first note of the call and is raised quickly to the peak or truck. Aboard ship only the first full eight measures of the call are used.

76. Motor Boat.—Routine—sounded as a signal to call away a motorboat. The particular motorboat desired may be designated by C-note blasts.

Quick ♩=200   MOTOR LAUNCH

77. Motor Launch.—**Routine**—sounded as a signal to call away a motor launch. The particular motor launch desired may be designated by C-note blasts.

♩=150   MOVING PICTURE CALL

78. Moving Picture Call.—**Routine**—this call is sounded five minutes before a moving picture is to begin.

(♩=100)   OFFICERS' CALL

79. Officer's Call.—**Routine**—sounded as a notification for all officers to report to the commanding officer or at some designated point. This call is also frequently employed as a signal for divisions to assemble at morning quarters for muster. In such cases it is sounded five minutes before assembly time.

(♩=132)   OUT SMOKING LAMP

80. Out Smoking Lamp.—**Routine**—sounded as a signal to knock off smoking.

(♩=152)   PAY CALL

81. Pay Call.—Routine—this call is sounded when the paymaster is ready to pay the crew and is a signal for the men to fall in at their proper places to receive their pay.

82. Provision Call.—Routine—sounded as a signal that provisions are about to be served. Also used as a signal to equip and provide boats for abandon ship.

83. Quick Time, March.—Routine—used as a signal to take up the quick step (120 paces to the minute) when on the march.

84. Race Boat Crew.—Routine—sounded as a signal to call away the race boat crew.

85. Rally by Companies.—Routine—sounded in the field to rally a company which has been dispersed.

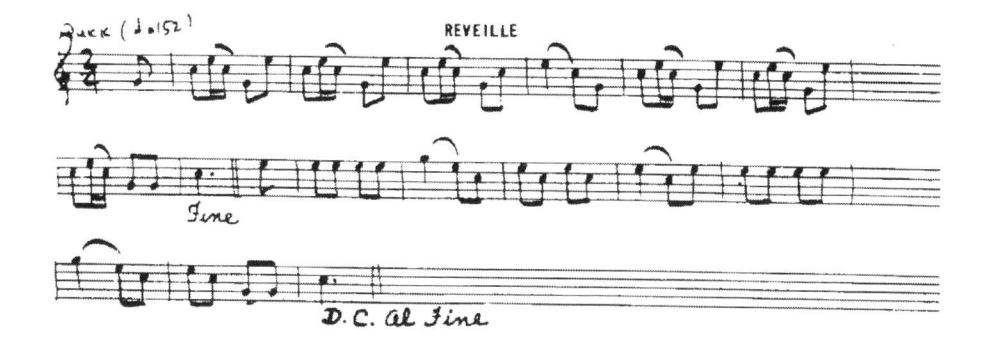

86. Reveille.—Routine—this familiar call is sounded to awaken all personnel for morning roll call. All Hands is piped immediately after the call is finished.

87. Right Oblique, March.—Routine—the first three notes are the preparatory command for a right oblique movement. The C-note blast is the command of execution and should be given as the right foot strikes the ground when the body of troops has reached the point where execution of the movement is to be made.

88. Route Step, March.—Routine—sounded as a signal on the march to take up the route step.

89. Saluting Gun Crews to Quarters.—Routine—sounded as a signal for saluting gun crews to make all necessary preparations to fire a salute.

90. School Call.—Routine—used either on board ship or at training stations to signal that classes are about to begin.

91. Secure.—Routine—sounded as a signal after battle or emergency drills to secure equipment.

92. Set Material Condition.—Emergency—sounded as a signal for all men to man their damage control stations. When followed by one E-note blast the call designates "set material condition able;" followed by two E-note blasts it indicates "set material condition baker."

93. Sick Call.—Routine—sounded at times designated by the commanding officer as a signal for men requiring routine medical attention to report to sick bay.

94. Surgeon's Party.—Routine—sounded as a signal for dressing station crews and battle stretcher men to muster at the sick bay for instruction in first aid.

95. Swimming Call.—Routine—sounded as a signal for the men taking part in swimming exercises to don their trunks and prepare for the swim.

96. Taps.—Routine—this beautiful and well-known call was written by General Daniel Butterfield and his brigade Bugler in July, 1862 to replace a previous, less melodious call. It is the last call to be sounded at night, with the exception of emergency calls, and is the signal for the men to turn in and extinguish unauthorized lights.

Taps is also sounded at the funeral of a member or ex-member of the armed services as the final military tribute to the service which that man has rendered to his country.

When a Bugler is to take part in a funeral service ashore he accompanies the firing party to the place of internment. Upon completion of the commitment service, the commander of the escort gives the command PRESENT ARMS. On this command, the bugler moves to the head of, and facing, the grave. When he has taken his position, he gives the hand salute without further command. At the command FIRE THREE VOLLEYS the firing party fires three volleys of blank cartridges and assumes the position of READY. Immediately following the last volley, the Bugler sounds Taps. Upon completion of the call, he again gives the hand salute, faces about, and rejoins his unit.

If for any reason the volleys are omitted from the ceremony, the Bugler follows the procedure described above, but sounds Taps immediately after moving to the head of the grave and giving the hand salute.

For burials at sea the Bugler falls in with the firing party. When the order "All hands bury the dead" is given, Officer's Call is sounded on the bugle. When the crew has assembled, Adjutant's Call is sounded and all divisions face the body. With the vessel hove to and the colors at half-mast the divisions are brought to Parade Rest for the reading of the scripture and for prayer. Upon conclusion of the prayers all divisions are brought to attention for the committal service by sounding Attention on the bugle. After the committal, three volleys are fired by the firing party, and the Bugler sounds Taps. Following this, benediction is said the colors are two-blocked. Retreat is sounded on the bugle to bring the ceremony to its close.

97. Tattoo.—Routine—Tattoo is sounded in the evening as a signal to make down bunks and prepare to retire. Aboard ship, Tattoo is a signal for silence about the decks. The origin of this call has been traced back to the Thirty Years War (1618-1648) when it was used by a German commander to call a halt to the nightly drinking bouts of his soldiers.

98. Torpedo Defense Fire-Control Exercise.—Routine—sounded as a signal for fire-control exercise, torpedo defense battery. When searchlights are to be included in the exercise, this call is followed by the call Man Searchlights.

99. Torpedo Defense Quarters.—**Emergency**—sounded as a signal at general quarters to call the torpedo defense gun crews from reserve.

100. To the Rear, March.—**Routine**—the first three measures serve as the preparatory command for this movement. The C-note blast is the command of execution and should be given as the right foot strikes the ground when the body of troops has reached the point where execution of the movement is to be made.

101. Watertight Doors.—**Routine and emergency**—sounded as a signal to secure the ship below the water line for the night during maneuvers or fog.

102. Whale Boat.—**Routine**—sounded as a signal to call away a whale boat. The particular whale boat desired may be designated by C-note blasts.

103. Wherry.—**Routine**—sounded as a signal to call away a wherry. The particular wherry desired may be designated by C-note blasts.

104. Working Party.—**Routine**—sounded as a signal for assembly of a working party.

Printed in Great Britain
by Amazon